FOR MATTHEW

ACKNOWLEDGMENTS
Thanks are due to the following:
Joseph Soukup for photograph page 2
Linton Whittles for photographs on endpapers and on pages 20 and 21
National Aeronautics and Space Administration for photograph on page 25

# The Lord's Prayer for Today

together with other
choice portions of
Holy Scripture ...

COMPILED AND ILLUSTRATED
BY ROYAL V. CARLEY

The C. R. Gibson Company, *Publishers*
Norwalk, Connecticut

Our Father which art
in heaven,

Whom have I in heaven but thee? and
there is none upon earth that I desire
beside thee.
My flesh and my heart faileth: but God
is the strength of my heart, and my
portion for ever.

*Psalm 73:25, 26*

God that made the world and all things
therein, seeing that he is Lord of heaven
and earth, dwelleth not in temples
made with hands;
Neither is worshipped with men's
hands, as though he needed any thing,
seeing he giveth to all life, and breath,
and all things;
And hath made of one blood all nations
of men for to dwell on all the face of
the earth, and hath determined the times
before appointed, and the bounds
of their habitation;
That they should seek the Lord, if haply
they might feel after him, and find
him, though he be not far from every
one of us:
For in him we live, and move, and
have our being . . .

*Acts 17: 24-28*

The Lord hath prepared his throne in
the heavens; and his kingdom ruleth
over all.
Bless the Lord, ye his angels, that excel
in strength, that do his commandments,
hearkening unto the voice of his word.
Bless ye the Lord, all ye his hosts;
ye ministers of his, that do his pleasure.
Bless the Lord, all his works in all places
of his dominion: bless the Lord,
O my soul.

*Psalm 103:19-22*

# Hallowed
# be thy name.

It is a good thing to give thanks unto the Lord,
and to sing praises unto thy name, O most High:
To shew forth thy lovingkindness in the morning,
and thy faithfulness every night,
Upon an instrument of ten strings, and upon the
psaltery; upon the harp with a solemn sound.
For thou, Lord, hast made me glad through thy
work: I will triumph in the works of thy hands.
O Lord, how great are thy works! and thy thoughts
are very deep.

*Psalm 92: 1-5*

I will be glad and rejoice in thee: I will sing praise
to thy name, O thou most High.

*Psalm 9:2*

Thy name, O Lord, endureth for ever; and thy
memorial, O Lord, throughout all generations.

*Psalm 135:13*

# Thy kingdom come.

Verily I say unto you, This generation shall not
pass, till all these things are fulfilled.

*Matthew 25:34*

And I heard a great voice out of heaven
saying, Behold, the tabernacle of God
is with men, and he will dwell with them,
and they shall be his people, and God
himself shall be with them, and be
their God.
And God shall wipe away all tears from
their eyes; and there shall be no more
death, neither sorrow, nor crying, neither
shall there be any more pain: for the
former things are passed away.

*Revelation 21:2-4*

Verily, verily, I say unto you, He that
heareth my word, and believeth on him
that sent me, hath everlasting life, and
shall not come into condemnation; but is
passed from death unto life.
Verily, verily, I say unto you, The hour is
coming, and now is, when the dead shall
hear the voice of the Son of God: and they
that hear shall live.
For as the Father hath life in himself;
so hath he given to the Son to have life
in himself;
And hath given him authority to execute
judgment also, because he is the
Son of man.

*John 5:24-27*

For the grace of God that bringeth
salvation hath appeared to all men,
Teaching us that, denying ungodliness and
wordly lusts, we should live soberly,
righteously, and godly, in this present
world;
Looking for that blessed hope, and the
glorious appearing of the great God and
our Saviour Jesus Christ.

*Titus 2:11-13*

# Thy will be done in earth, as it is in heaven.

For I came down from heaven, not to do mine own will, but the will of him that sent me.
And this is the Father's will which hath sent me, that of all which he hath given me I should lose nothing, but should raise it up again at the last day.
And this is the will of him that sent me, that every one which seeth the Son, and believeth on him, may have everlasting life: and I will raise him up at the last day.

*John 6:38-40*

Teach me to do thy will; for thou art my God: thy spirit is good; lead me into the land of uprightness.

*Psalm 143:10*

O Lord, thou has searched me, and known me.
Thou knowest my downsitting and mine uprising, thou understandest my thought afar off.
Thou compassest my path and my lying down, and are acquainted with all my ways.
For there is not a word in my tongue, but lo, O Lord, thou knowest it altogether.
Thou hast beset me behind and before, and laid thine hand upon me.
Such knowledge is too wonderful for me; it is high, I cannot attain unto it.

*Psalm 139:1-6*

God . . . Who will have all men to be saved, and to come unto the knowledge of the truth.

*I Timothy 2:4*

Then said Jesus unto his disciples, If any man will come after me, let him deny himself, and take up his cross, and follow me.

*Matthew 16:24*

# Give us this day our daily bread.

And he said unto his disciples, Therefore I say unto you, Take no thought for your life, what ye shall eat; neither for the body, what ye shall put on.

The life is more than meat, and the body is more than raiment.

Consider the ravens: for they neither sow nor reap; which neither have storehouse nor barn; and God feedeth them: how much more are ye better than the fowls?

And which of you with taking thought can add to his stature one cubit? If ye then be not able to do that thing

which is least, why take ye thought for the rest?

Consider the lilies how they grow: they toil not, they spin not; and yet I say unto you, that Solomon in all his glory was not arrayed like one of these.

If then God so clothe the grass, which is to day in the field, and to morrow is cast into the oven; how much more will he clothe you, o ye of little faith?

And seek not ye what ye shall eat, or what ye shall drink, neither be ye of doubtful mind.

For all these things do the nations of the world seek after: and your Father knoweth that ye have need of these things.

But rather seek ye the kingdom of God; and all these things shall be added unto you.

*Luke 12: 22-31*

# And forgive us our trespasses, as we forgive those who trespass against us.

Come now, and let us reason together, saith the Lord: though your sins be as scarlet, they shall be as white as snow; though they be red like crimson, they shall be as wool.

*Isaiah 1:18*

If we confess our sins, he is faithful and just to forgive us our sins, and to cleanse us from all unrighteousness.

*I John 1:9*

. . . be ye kind one to another, tenderhearted, forgiving one another, even as God for Christ's sake hath forgiven you.

*Ephesians 4:32*

If my people, which are called by
my name, shall humble themselves,
and pray, and seek my face, and turn
from their wicked ways; then
will I hear from heaven, and will
forgive their sin, and will heal
their land.

*II Chronicles 7:14*

Then came Peter to him, and said,
Lord, how oft shall my brother sin
against me, and I forgive him?
till seven times?
Jesus saith unto him, I say not unto
thee, Until seven times: but,
Until seventy times seven.

*Matthew 18:21, 22*

And when ye stand praying, forgive,
if ye have ought against any:
that your Father also which is in
heaven may forgive you your
trespasses.

*Mark 11:25*

Thou shalt not avenge, nor bear any
grudge against the children of thy
people, but thou shalt love thy
neighbor as thyself: I am the Lord.

*Leviticus 19:18*

# And lead us not into temptation,

O Lord, I know that the way of man is not in himself:
it is not in man that walketh to direct his steps.

*Jeremiah 10:23*

The steps of a good man are ordered by the Lord:
and he delighteth in his way.
Though he fall, he shall not be utterly cast down:
for the Lord upholdeth him with his hand.

*Psalm 37:23, 24*

Draw me not away with the wicked, and with the workers of iniquity, which speak peace to their neighbours, but mischief is in their hearts.

*Psalm 28:3*

There hath no temptation taken you but such as is common to man: but God is faithful, who will not suffer you to be tempted above that ye are able; but will with the temptation also make a way to escape, that ye may be able to bear it.

*I Corinthians 10:13*

For thou art my rock and my fortress; therefore for thy name's sake lead me, and guide me.

*Psalm 31:3*

Lead me in thy truth, and teach me: for thou art the God of my salvation; on thee do I wait all the day.

*Psalm 25:5*

And he said unto me, My grace is sufficient for thee: for my strength is made perfect in weakness.

*II Corinthians 12:9*

# but deliver us from evil:

Grace be to you and peace from God
the Father, and from our Lord
Jesus Christ,
Who gave himself for our sins, that
he might deliver us from this
present evil world, according to the
will of God and our Father:
To whom be glory for ever and ever.
Amen.

*Galatians 1:3-5*

Wherefore take unto you the whole
armour of God, that ye may be able
to withstand in the evil day, and
having done all, to stand.
Stand therefore, having your loins
girt about with truth, and having on
the breastplate of righteousness;
And your feet shod with the
preparation of the gospel of peace;
Above all, taking the shield of faith,
wherewith ye shall be able to
quench all the fiery darts of the
wicked.
And take the helmet of salvation,
and the sword of the Spirit, which
is the word of God:
Praying always with all prayer and
supplication in the Spirit, and
watching thereunto with all
perseverance and supplication for
all saints.

*Ephesians 6:13-18*

But the Lord is faithful, who shall
stablish you, and keep you from
evil.

*II Thessalonians 3:3*

# For thine is the kingdom,

Then shall the King say unto them on his right hand, Come, ye blessed of my Father, inherit the kingdom prepared for you from the foundation of the world.
*Matthew 25:34*

Therefore are they before the throne of God, and serve him day and night in his temple: and he that sitteth on the throne shall dwell among them.
They shall hunger no more, neither thirst any more; neither shall the sun light on them, nor any heat.
For the Lamb which is in the midst of the throne shall feed them, and shall lead them unto living fountains of waters: and God shall wipe away all tears from their eyes.
*Revelation 7:15-17*

. . . an inheritance incorruptible, and undefiled, and that fadeth not away, reserved in heaven for you,
Who are kept by the power of God through faith unto salvation ready to be revealed in the last time.
*I Peter 1:4, 5*

Then shall the righteous shine forth as the sun in the kingdom of their Father. Who hath ears to hear, let him hear.

*Matthew 13:43*

Giving thanks unto the Father, which hath made us meet to be partakers of the inheritance of the saints in light:

Who hath delivered us from the power of darkness, and hath translated us into the kingdom of his dear Son:

In whom we have redemption through his blood, even the forgiveness of sins:

*Colossians 1:12, 13, 14*

Hearken, my beloved brethren, Hath not God chosen the poor of this world rich in faith, and heirs of the kingdom which he hath promised to them that love him?

*James 2:5*

# and the power,

He hath made the earth by his power, he hath
established the world by his wisdom, and hath
stretched out the heavens by his discretion. When
he uttereth his voice, there is a multitude of waters
in the heavens, and he causeth the vapours to ascend
from the ends of the earth; he maketh lightnings
with rain, and bringeth forth the wind out of
his treasures.

*Jeremiah 10:12, 13*

For by him were all things created, that are in heaven, and that are in earth, visible and invisible, whether they be thrones, or dominions, or principalities, or powers: all things were created by him, and for him: And he is before all things, and by him all things consist.

*Colossians 1:16*

The Lord reigneth, he is clothed with majesty; the Lord is clothed with strength, wherewith he hath girded himself: the world also is stablished, that it cannot be moved.

*Psalm 93:1*

# and the glory,

Thine, O Lord, is the greatness, and the power, and
the glory, and the victory, and the majesty: for all
that is in the heaven and in the earth is thine;
thine is the kingdom, O Lord, and thou art exalted as
head above all.
Both riches and honour come of thee, and thou
reignest over all; and in thine hand is power and
might; and in thine hand it is to make great, and to
give strength unto all.

*I Chronicles 29:11, 12*

The heavens declare the glory of God; and the
firmament sheweth his handywork.
Day unto day uttereth speech; and night unto night
sheweth knowledge.

*Psalm 19:1, 2*

# for ever.

Before the mountains were brought forth, or ever thou hadst formed the earth and the world, even from everlasting to everlasting, thou art God.

*Psalm 90:2*

And he shewed me a pure river of water of life, clear as crystal, proceeding out of the throne of God and of the Lamb.
In the midst of the street of it, and on either side of the river, was there the tree of life, which bare twelve manner of fruits, and yielded her fruit every month: and the leaves of the tree were for the healing of the nations.
And there shall be no more curse: but the throne of God and of the Lamb shall be in it; and his servants shall serve him:
And they shall see his face; and his name shall be in their foreheads.
And there shall be no night there; and they need no candle, neither light of the sun; for the Lord God giveth them light: and they shall reign for ever and ever.

*Revelation 22:1-5*

In my Father's house are many mansions: if it were not so, I would have told you. I go to prepare a place for you.
And if I go and prepare a place for you, I will come again, and receive you unto myself; that where I am, there ye may be also.

*John 14:2, 3*

Blessed be the God and Father of our Lord Jesus Christ, which according to his abundant mercy hath begotten us again unto a lively hope by the resurrection of Jesus Christ from the dead.

*I Peter 1:3*

Amen.